ON ECSTASY

Barrie Kosky

MELBOURNE
UNIVERSITY
PRESS

MELBOURNE UNIVERSITY PRESS
An imprint of Melbourne University Publishing Limited
187 Grattan Street, Carlton, Victoria 3053, Australia
mup-info@unimelb.edu.au
www.mup.com.au

First published 2008
Text © Barrie Kosky, 2008
Design and typography © Melbourne University Publishing Ltd, 2008

Text design by Alice Graphics
Cover design by Nada Backovic Designs
Typeset by Midland Typesetters, Australia
Printed in Australia by Griffin Press, SA

National Library of Australia Cataloguing-in-Publication entry

Kosky, Barrie.
On ecstasy / Barrie Kosky.

ISBN 9780522855340 (hbk.)

Ecstasy.

152.42

For my grandmothers, Leah and Magda.
They don't make them like that anymore.

Ecstasy:

1. Intense joy or delight.
2. A state of emotion so intense that one is carried away beyond rational thought and self-control.
3. The trance, frenzy or rapture associated with mystic or prophetic exaltation.

Middle English *extasie*, from Old French, from Late Latin *extasis* (terror), from Greek *ekstasis* (astonishment, distraction), from *existani* (to displace, derange). *Ek* (out of) + *Histanai* (to place).

It is not necessary that you leave the house.
Remain at your table and listen.
Do not even listen, only wait.
Do not even wait, be wholly still and alone.
The world will present itself to you for its
unmasking, it has no choice, in ecstasy it will
writhe at your feet.

Franz Kafka

I

In the beginning, there was no smell. She simply cut the carrots, onions, parsnips and celery into pieces and threw them over the raw chicken. I never liked that raw chicken sitting dead and motionless in that big saucepan. Didn't like it. Didn't trust it. I was always happy when the vegetables were thrown in and the water was poured over the dead chook, drowning it forever. There was nothing to smell and certainly, nothing to taste. I had to wait for that. A whole twenty-four hours of waiting, waiting, waiting.

Any serious connoisseur of chicken soup will tell you that the Chicken Soup Ritual is divided into three distinct and clear sections: Preparation. Expectation. Consumption. Any 7-year-old Jewish child will tell you that Preparation and Expectation are infuriating, tortuous obstacles to Consumption. Is it finished yet? That big saucepan with that big lid boiling that strange brew of chunky veggies and dead chook. Is it finished yet? The steam emerging from under the lid of the saucepan, as if my Uncle Sol were sitting underneath the lid, blowing out his cigar smoke. Is it finished yet? Whack, as my grandmother's hand slapped my paws away from the stove.

My Polish grandmother made a chicken soup like no other chicken soup. To this day, to my knowledge and experience, it has never been bettered. She made a chopped liver that melted in your mouth, she made a gefilte fish that bounced for days on your tongue, she made a chocolate cake the likes of which Western cuisine will never, ever taste again; but her chicken soup surpassed even the superlatives of these creations. Her chicken soup was the Caravaggio of soups. The Rainer Maria Rilke of soups. The Arturo Benedetti Michelangeli of soups.

But we are not there yet. We are a long, long way from Consumption. And didn't

I know it. After a couple of hours, my grandmother tilted the saucepan over a big glass bowl and poured the liquid into it. And what a liquid, oh, what a liquid. Gold, like Howard Carter glimpsed when he saw wonderful things through the hole in Tutankhamen's tomb. Gold, like the wheels on my grandfather's Bechstein piano I used to sit under and rub, in the hope that the gold would come off on my hands. Gold, like the box on my Hungarian grandmother's mantelpiece, where her bridge cards lay waiting for the ladies who lunch. It was a Nile, an Amazon, a Euphrates of liquid gold heaven. But it was not yet mine.

The fridge door slammed shut and I was told, as always, not to disturb the soup, which my grandmother said was sleeping. Sleeping soup. Every now and then I would sneak a peek to see if there was any change in the bowl. I was always shocked to witness the transformation next day of the once sparkling, golden liquid into darkish wobbly sludge. How could something that smelt so incredible and looked so dazzling end up, twenty-four hours later, like miserable brown jelly? I just didn't get it.

What I did get, however, was the beginning of part three of the ritual: Consumption. If I had been a good boy, done my homework, practised the piano and washed my hands, my grandmother would let me slowly scrape the white, congealed fat off the top of the soup. I loved this part. With the skill, patience and dexterity of a plastic surgeon, I removed the thick layer of fat with a wooden spoon, making sure not to pierce the skin of the dark sludge underneath.

My grandmother would ladle the brown slop into a saucepan and tell me to get out of the kitchen. Sit. Wait. It was unbearable. I wanted to scream. Sometimes I did. Like the famous Chicken Soup Tantrum of 1977. Is it finished yet? And there, before my eyes, it appeared. The Chicken Soup.

That first spoonful, as the hot soup washed in my mouth and glided down my throat, was intense, cosmic rapture. The second spoonful. Bliss. The third spoonful. Transcendental bliss. The Chicken Soup Room at the end of Kubrick's *2001*. A soup that took you to the beginning and end of time itself. A dazzling, pure, clear Rhapsody in Gold.

A young boy in a brown cowboy hat skips down a steep, dry embankment. He is playing a silver flute. The young boy is called Jimmy. The silver flute is called Freddy. The flute also talks. Jimmy and Freddy jump into a big, beautiful, brightly coloured boat and sail off over the sparkling water.

It is 4 p.m. A cold, miserable afternoon in suburban Melbourne. 1974. I am seven years old and sitting on the brown shagpile carpet of our living room in front of the television. Sitting, as I have been for weeks, every day at 4 p.m. Well, 3.52 p.m. to be more precise. Just to be on the safe side, you know. In case I missed it. I couldn't miss it. I never missed it. It was what I had waited the whole day to see. It was the highlight of my waking hours. It was Jack Wild's wet jeans in the opening credits of *HR Pufnstuf*.

They were wet. Very wet. And they were tight. Very tight. I remember two distinct images: the first, as he lay on his stomach, motionless on the sandy river bank with the water clinging to those tight, wet jeans; and the second, as he was dragged up onto his feet by the Mayor of Living Island, HR Pufnstuf, and his two midget Rescue Rangers, Kling and Klang. Jack Wild shook the water from his thick, black hair, and his clothes clung to his body. Wet and tight.

Jack Wild was seventeen when he made the series, but he looked much younger. I was intoxicated with the show. Intoxicated with the colours of the sets and outlandish costumes, intoxicated with the funky, groovy, toe-tapping music, intoxicated with all those singing and dancing houses, trees, animals and clocks. But there was something else at work when those dark, wet jeans flashed across the screen. Another sensation. A strange, new sensation. It frightened me, this feeling. It unbalanced me. I only felt it when I saw the way the wet jeans clung to his legs and to his backside. I sat there, a cross-legged, bespectacled seven year old in a Melbourne Grammar uniform, holding my breath, sinking into the shagpile with a feeling of palpitating, delicious nausea.

I didn't like Jack Wild. I liked his wet jeans but I didn't like him. He was irritating, silly, annoying. Like one of those irritating, silly, annoying boys from school. Pointless. Didn't get him. After the opening credits, he bored me. But I was never, ever bored by Witchiepoo. I loved Witchiepoo. I loved everything about her: her fabulous flying broomstick (the Vroom-Broom), her fabulous vaudeville make-up, her fabulous red hair, her fabulous multi-coloured stockings, her fabulous false nose and her fabulous goofy henchmen, Orson and Seymour. Why didn't I have friends like that?

I loved Witchiepoo and I wanted to be Witchiepoo. I wanted to zap my magic wand and make people disappear. I wanted to wear big, red sunglasses and sing 'Oranges, Poranges: Who says there ain't no rhyme for oranges!' I wanted to live in a dilapidated gothic palace and watch people through a big, silver telescope. No, forget Jack Wild and his tight, wet buttocks, I wanted to have big red hair, sing, and dance and ride a Vroom-Broom.

I had no problem in combining my love of Witchiepoo with my strange *sehnsucht* for Jack's jeans. It seemed a natural part of my 30-minute afternoon ritual. The shag-pile was my magic carpet, and for half an hour I hovered in a parallel universe. God help my brother or sister if they interrupted me. This was my ritual and before the days of VCR. If I missed the moment, I'd missed the moment. But I never missed the moment. Seeing all those images before my eyes, watching them dissolve, split, merge, evaporate and multiply was unlike any other feeling I had previously experienced. All other experiences were measured against it.

Jack's wet jeans made me breathless. Witchiepoo made me exhilarated. Then, sadness at 4.30 p.m. It was all over for another day. I moped around the house after the show had finished. Unable to concentrate. Unable to comprehend the joy or the sadness. I only managed to rouse myself from this lethargy with the bat-squeak of excitement that flushed through my body when I thought about tomorrow. Yes, tomorrow. Tomorrow at 4 o'clock. Wet jeans and big noses all over again.

Around the same time that Jack, Witchiepoo and chicken soup entered my life, my Hungarian grandmother presented me with a stack of records. I was a little confused, and unsure of them. My other records had shiny, new covers with stuffed animals or cartoon characters on them. But my grandmother's records were old and stained. They were bright yellow, with a weird-looking woman staring out at me from the cover.

My grandmother explained that she wanted me to listen to these records because in a few months she was going to take me somewhere special. Where? Just wait. What? Just listen to the music. Why? Because you need to prepare yourself.

Prepare myself? I had no idea what she was talking about, but I rushed to the record-player and put one of the records on. I winced at the cacophony. The record was scratched and the music crackled through the speakers. I took it off and tried another record. More cacophony. More scratch. More crackle. This time lots of voices were singing together. It was all too confusing. I took it off and tried the third record, expecting just scratching and crackling. But this time I was surprised. A soft, high voice. A sound I had never heard before. The voice was strange. It floated through the air, yet also cut through it. Sliced it. Went higher and higher and suddenly, without any warning, plunged downwards and became darker, deeper, scarier.

A man tried to sing along, but I didn't like that. I wanted the lady's voice again.

And I wanted her by herself, not with the bleating sheep. I put the needle back at the beginning of the record where I had first heard the lady's voice. And I listened again. Needle off. Needle on. And again. Needle off. Needle on. And again. Who was the lady? Why did she sing like this? And why did her voice caress my skin, sink into my flesh and whirl around in the middle of my stomach? And what was she singing about? And why did she sound so sad? And why did I like it?

My grandmother explained the mystery. The records were called *Madam Butterfly*, the singer was a lady called Renate Tebaldi, and this was a recording of something we would see in a few months. I still didn't get it. How could we see what she sang?

For the next few months I listened to this *Madam Butterfly*. I had no idea of the story, or the characters, or the words. I didn't like it when they all sang together, I hated it when the men sang and I got really bored when only the orchestra played. But when the lady with the high voice sang I was transfixed. I kept on trying to connect the weird-looking woman on the record sleeve with the voice. It wasn't a photograph from a production or even a photograph of a singer. It was a brutal, geometric, graphic rendering of a Japanese woman. My grandmother told me that she was called Madam Butterfly. But she didn't look like a butterfly to me and anyway, she seemed to have nothing to do with the voice that filled the living room.

I played it louder and louder. I sped it up so she sounded like a chipmunk. I slowed it down so she sounded like an old man. But I still liked her best when I played her on normal speed. Who was this weird and wonderful Madam Butterfly? And when were we going to meet her?

After what seemed like an eternity, the night arrived. My grandmother had finally given me a brief rundown of the story but I had no idea what she was talking about. All far too complicated. She told me not to worry, to just enjoy the music, the sets, the costumes. I had been to the theatre before, so the delicious experience of sitting in a dark room with total strangers watching people whirl in front of me was not new. What was new, however, was that later

I could recall, in vivid detail, the experience. The strange ladies, all in those funny white dresses; the cherry blossom floating through the light and falling all over the stage; the weird but beautiful paper umbrellas (Could I have one, Nana?) everyone kept twirling and floating; and through all this exotic dream, that lady's voice, vibrating through the Princess Theatre, caressing my eardrums, entering my body and making me dizzy.

That night, as I lay tucked up under my grandmother's goose-feather eiderdown, she finished off the night as she always did, with a Grimm's fairy story. She had a thick Hungarian accent, so it was a little like being read to by Béla Lugosi in drag. The stories terrified me. Her voice terrified me. After she had finished, turned out the light and left the room, I lay trembling under the eiderdown. But that night, I was not alone. Madam Butterfly sang to me again. Her voice came back to me, soft and beautiful, like an echo of an echo of an echo. And I fell asleep.

I hated sport. I hated winter sport. I hated my German teacher, Fritz Dobberstein, who coached the soccer team. 'Schnell, Kosky. Schnell!!!' he would scream as I meandered, bored out of my brain, towards the ball. Fritz's face would turn blutwurst red and I would pretend I hadn't heard. I hated the wet grass. I hated the meaninglessness of it all. I hated my gawky, unformed pubescent body and I hated how they made us play in the rain and how the rain ran down my glasses and how I couldn't see anything or anybody.

But all was forgiven a few minutes later. Especially if the older boys were there. The two hours of sadistic soccer were transformed instantly into the olfactory spice bazaar that was the Melbourne Grammar School Changing Rooms.

The changing rooms were not for me a place of voyeurism. That would come later in my adolescence, where the glimpse of a footballer's thigh or a hockey player's navel was enough to send me clutching for my pearls. No, early on, it was all about the smell. It wasn't about looking. It wasn't about touching. Years later, when I visited Istanbul for the first

time and found myself lost in the labyrin-
thine passages of the spice bazaar, where
the contrapuntal confusion of spices,
herbs and fruits steamed up my nostrils,
I thought back to those changing rooms.
Different smells, but the same sensation,
where your nostrils burn and glow and
you can taste the smell on your tongue,
your lips, your skin. Not one smell, not
two or three but a profusion of conflict-
ing smells so intense that it was like
snorting a Scriabin symphony.

Body odour of every imaginable flavour,
sweat, socks, Dencorub, hot water, cheap
soap, the wet old wood of the lockers. All
clashing in my nostrils, all fighting to get
up my nasal cavities. Whirling in my nostrils like a thousand miniature tornadoes.

Sometimes it became so overwhelming I really thought that I was going to faint, or vomit or scream. Forget cocaine or pharmaceutical stimulants; the smells of the Melbourne Grammar School Changing Rooms were the most intense thing that's ever been up my nose.

I usually stayed until everyone had left. First, because I didn't like to change in front of the other boys, and second, because it allowed me to experience the changing rooms as an empty temple. I was an ancient Israelite priest entering the Holy of Holies in the Temple in Jerusalem. A sacred space charged with more smells than the Chanel laboratory. A forbidden zone touched with rapture. My Holy of Holies.

My father's fur empire was located in a large warehouse in Richmond. My grandfather and his brothers and sisters had arrived in Australia from Russia just after the revolution. My father ran the entire business now, but two women managed the upstairs and downstairs. Upstairs was the domain of my Auntie Eda: round, tiny, Russian and with Very Big Hair. Downstairs was the domain of my grandmother, Leah: round, tiny, Polish and with Very Big Hair. Auntie Eda did the books and the office, Granny Leah did the cutting and pattern sewing. I never liked upstairs, although I did like Auntie Eda, despite the fact that she made the worst-tasting matzo balls in the history of Judaism. Downstairs was a different matter.

A vast field of fur coats packed the ground floor. Hundreds and hundreds of coats. Mink, kangaroo, possum, sheep. You name it—it died and hung on a rack in Richmond. The coats were arranged in a particular order: cheap through to luxury. Cheap was at the front, and way down the back, through rack after rack of dead animal, was the luxury section. Mink coat after mink coat after mink coat.

I had just been given the Narnia books and I was obsessed. Later in life, I came to loathe the Narnia books, particularly when I eventually found out what they were all about, but as a 7-year-old boy with a feverish imagination and overstimulated sensory perceptions, I desperately wanted to go through my own wardrobe and to find my snow-covered hills on the other side of somewhere. That big lion and that thin witch you could keep (although I was rather keen on the Turkish Delight she kept in her sleigh) but the wardrobe was another matter. That wardrobe and those old fur coats the children found on their way through to Narnia fuelled my little head with breathtaking intensity.

So, it was no surprise that after reading about how to get to the mystical kingdom, I was standing in the middle of my father's mink coats, determined that somewhere in between all this black and brown skinned rodent was my entrance to Narnia. I loved being there. I loved turning out the fluorescent lights and plunging myself into darkness. The journey began but soon

I forgot about my quest to discover snow and Turkish Delight, for I found more delight in touching.

Running my fingers along the mink. Tracing the outline of the long coats from the collar to the hem. Softly rubbing the arm of the coat against my face so that soft mink prickled my cheek and my chin. Rubbing the mink against my lips. Then, I would crawl under a long coat and experience my next sensation: the silk lining. I cocooned myself inside the coat so I was enveloped in silk. It was cool against my face, like a silk sorbet after the heat of the mink.

For hours and hours I played alone in the dark forest of mink coats. I lost myself. I surrendered to drowning in a sea of dark fur, and when I emerged, there was no snow, no sleigh, no Narnia. Only my grandmother, with her tape measure around her neck, pins in her mouth and her feet whirling on the Singer sewing machine.

And rows and rows and rows of lonely fur coats.

II

A symphony must be like the world.
It must contain everything.

Gustav Mahler

Fifty-six bars of a 7-octave string hum. A landscape at once spacious, full of possibilities and eternal. Distant brass fanfares punctuate the hum, like the past calling out, defiantly and courageously, from a long-forgotten tower in a long-forgotten castle. A cuckoo calls, piercing the air. A snaky, winding chromatic phrase for the strings glides through the landscape, seducing and menacing. And always, those sad falling fourths, dotted through the world, like sighing ghosts.

I was fifteen when I heard Mahler for the first time. Nothing had prepared me for this. What was this music? What were these sounds? And why, oh why, despite its strange and alien nature, did I feel I had heard this music before? Somewhere, somehow in some half-remembered dream.

If I was dumbstruck by the musical vocabulary of the first movement of Mahler's First Symphony, nothing could have prepared me for the sounds of the third movement. Boom Boom. Boom

Boom. The funeral march starts. Boom Boom. The timpani, almost imperceptible. Like giant's feet wrapped in cotton wool. The double bass starts playing 'Frère Jacques' in a minor key. A double-bass solo? 'Frère Jacques'? As a funeral march? A children's song that asks the question 'Are you sleeping, Brother Jack?' played as a mournful, funereal canon? I was gobsmacked. As the orchestra played on I saw that little child's hearse going down that empty, muddy road. Then Mahler gives the listener one of his most wondrous inventions: in the middle of the 'Frère Jacques' funeral march appears a klezmer band. Yes, Uncle Maurie's bar mitzvah band strikes up in the orchestra as if a group of musicians had just planted themselves in the middle of the peak-hour traffic.

What sort of a composer puts a funeral march to a children's nursery song and a zippy village klezmer band on the same page of a symphonic score? This music seduced me. It took me, convulsed me and drowned me. It suffocated me. It was gorgeous, repellent, terrifying. It scared the shit out of me. It still does. Boom Boom. Boom Boom. Frère Jacques, Frère Jacques, dormez-vous, dormez-vous? What was that Jewish band doing there, anyway? And that scraping, high, double-bass solo at the beginning of the movement. So wrong and yet so right. A senile man with emphysema in a children's playground.

The finale of the First Symphony exploded through my bedroom, shattering to pieces everything that had been heard before those exultant brass fanfares, once an echo in the first movement, now blaringly present and real; the plodding bass ostinato, the thrilling outpouring of unquenchable, radiant joy. And those whooping brass ejaculations at the end of the movement, stopped only by those unexpected brutal chords at the end, slammed down like punctuation marks. All of these sounds were new to me. Their excessive, overpowering force overwhelmed me. I felt exhilarated and seasick. I was riding a rollercoaster in the Atlantic.

I listened to this music for months and even used it for the very first theatre production I directed. A teacher at school had recommended to me that I should have a go at directing. So I took myself

off to the school library and found a tat-
tered copy of a play called *Woyzeck*, by
some German guy. I had been rehearsing
my all-male production of the play for a
few weeks when I decided that what the
murder scene needed was a good dose of
Mahler. So, as my boy Woyzeck slit the
throat of his lover, Marie, I played the
third movement underneath the scene.
Boom Boom. Slit. Boom Boom. Slit. Frère
Jacques, Frère Jacques, dormez-vous,
dormez-vous? Slit. Scream. Buckets of
blood. Every time I hear that music I see
my mother's kitchen knife (borrowed for
the show) scraping across the throat of
an adolescent boy in a black dress. Boom
Boom. Boom Boom. Slit.

I am hitting myself against the wall,
but the walls are giving way.

Gustav Mahler

Mahler wrote no operas. He didn't have to. As Leonard Bernstein once said, every one of his symphonies 'behaves like an opera'. His grasp of coup-de-théâtre, of character, of scenery, of dramatic confrontation, of lighting, of aural mise-en-scène, is unequalled in symphonic composition. His music is populated by shadows, armies, skeletons, marching bands, funeral processions, figures pulled from a Brueghel marketplace, a Bosch garden, a Bacon bathroom. His music transfigures, it warps, it defies symmetry, it induces vertigo, claustrophobia and neurosis. It soothes and comforts. It hurts.

In 1910, Mahler sought the psycho-analytical advice of Sigmund Freud. His sessions took the form of a long, 4-hour walk around the streets of Vienna. Mahler recounted an anecdote to Freud from his childhood. He had been born into a Jewish family in the small town of Iglau in Moravia. His parents argued frequently and ferociously. One day, the young Gustav ran out of the house to escape the furious battle. As he ran into the street in front of his house, he heard a barrel organ playing a popular song, 'Ach, du lieber Augustin'. As Freud noted much later: 'In Mahler's opinion the conjunction of high tragedy and light amusement was from then on inextricably fixed in his mind'.

Tragedy and amusement. That's what I experienced when I watched Leonard Bernstein leading the New York Philharmonic in a performance of the Second Symphony. The applause had barely subsided when Lenny swung and struck his down beat. The paw of a feral, silver-haired tiger claiming its first meal of the day. For the next ninety minutes I sat transfixed. The music shuddered and lurched. Lenny crouched and jumped into the air. The music floated in a cloud of nostalgic sweetness. Lenny swayed in a trance, swung around, pirouetted. The music spread out into a vast, exultant radiance. Lenny seemed to grow a few feet taller.

He stood in front of that huge army of musicians and singers, a man standing in front of the sun, determined to redirect its course.

I watched the dybbuk of Mahler's music enter into this man's body. The music entered into him and emerged again, transfigured. He was Leah the bride to Mahler's Kabbalah. And when the chorus shouted their defiant 'Bereite dich zu leben!' (Prepare thyself to live!) his body seemed to take on an almost superhuman intensity. Mahler's struggle became Lenny's struggle.

Oh Schmerz! Du Alldurchdringer!
Dir bin ich entrungen.
O Tod! Du Allbezwinger
Nun bist du bezwungen!

Mit Flügel, die ich mir errungen,
In heissen Liebesstreben
Werd ich entschweben
Zum Licht, zu dem kein Aug
    gedrungen!

(Oh, all-piercing pain,
From you I have been wrested!
Oh, all-conquering death,
Now you are conquered.

With wings that I have gained
Shall I soar aloft
In love's ardent striving
To the light to which no eye has
    pierced.)

Lenny as Supernova. Well, certainly a
schwitzing Supernova; I had never seen so

much sweat fly off a human body. At the magnificent climax of the last movement, he resembled nothing less than a mad penguin doing an impression of a sprinkler system. Watching him was an amazing experience for a 16-year-old schoolboy. I had never seen a body wrenched with so much torment, joy and passion. Mahler's ambivalent Jewish-Christian Nietzschean agnostic personality found a living, breathing, sweating counterpart in Bernstein's muscles, bones and flesh. I was electrified. Did music really have the power to do this to a human body? Did he have control over it? What was being released within this man's body? And who or what was providing the impetus for all of this unbridled ecstasy?

Mahler wrote, when he was describing the scherzo of the Second Symphony:

> When you wake out of this sad dream, and must re-enter life, confused as it is, it happens easily that this always stirring, never-resting, never-comprehensible pushing that is life becomes *horrible* to you, like the notion of dancing figures in a brightly lit ballroom, into which you are peering from outside, in the dark night—from such a *distance* that you can *not* hear the music they dance to. Then life seems meaningless to you, like a horrible chimera, that you wrench yourself out with a horrible cry of dissent.

For all the rapturous majesty of the last movement of the Second Symphony, it seemed, at the end when Lenny stood there, drenched in his own sweat and tears, more like that chimera that Mahler described. That horrible cry of dissent. Wow, I thought. I want to be a conductor.

So, I became a conductor. My orchestras came from London, Dresden, Cleveland, Berlin. My audiences were swept up in my lacerating Mahler performances and my bedroom became my private concert hall, my private fetish salon. I was so obsessed with Mahler's music that in my brief but spectacular career as a leading inter-national bedroom conductor, he was the only composer whose music I conducted. I pounded through the Second, expansively drove my way through the Third and usu-ally at 5.22 p.m. on most afternoons, I was dancing with the angels. When I discovered the Eighth Symphony, nothing could hold me back.

I raised my plastic chopstick (it was the closest thing I could find in the kitchen) and the Royal Concertgebouw Orchestra and a chorus of thousands jubilantly proclaimed 'Ven: creator spiritus', and an LP and a half later I was leading the chorus in the hushed tones of 'Alles Vergängliche ist nur ein Gleichnis'. The whole bedroom vibrated. The entire universe was rotating in it. My bedroom was Big Bang. More often than not, I was interrupted by someone telling me to turn the volume down or that dinner was ready or that the neighbours were complaining. But I didn't care. Up went the volume. Up went the decibels of the orchestra. Up went the soaring phrases of the choir. There was no way that this maestro was going to sit down for lamb chops until my plastic chopstick had finished with the angels.

III

*When we speak the word 'life', it must
be understood we are not referring to life
as we know it from its surface of fact,
but to that fragile, fluctuating centre which
forms never reach.*

Antonin Artaud

I first really explored the idea of ecstatic theatre in my production of *The Dybbuk*. I had been drawn to Anski's text initially because of his powerful and hypnotic combination of religious ritual, horror and a damn good classic love story. But as I rehearsed the production in the freezing cold of an abandoned inner-city Melbourne warehouse, something else began to emerge and take hold of me.

Maybe it was all those late-night rehearsals when the space was lit by only one small lamp, sending our shadows flickering all over the walls as we worked. Maybe it was the Yiddish and Hebrew songs floating through the darkness. Maybe it was too much chicken schnitzel from Café Scheherazade, which I con-sumed on a near daily basis.

The actor emerged, dressed as a yeshiva bokher, crippled and emaciated from the darkness. He was bent low with a small prayer book on his back. We put steel caps on the soles of his shoes so that as he shuffled along the concrete, his feet scraped like a sick cat. He stopped and proceeded to eat, slowly and methodically, page after page of his prayer book. Word after word of Hebrew text he put in his mouth, chewed and swallowed. It had begun. The process of consumption, the consumption of a text from the prophecies of Ezekiel, resulted in a physical manifestation of rapture. Ezekiel saw wheels within wheels; these images were eaten by the young student who in turn saw visions of God. Later in the play, the young student articulates his vision as he describes what he has seen in the hidden sentences, words and letters of the mystical texts:

> Between its covers I have had glimpses of rooms, chambers and corridors in the palace of God ... I have enfolded my heart in the pages of the Kabbalah and my heart has burst into flames ... eyes within eyes have opened wide ... I have seen the edges of the great, dark curtain slowly lift.

Transcendental religious revelation, ecstatic self-immolation and the rising of the all-knowing, all-revealing Ur-theatre curtain. And all in the one vision! *The Dybbuk* contains two great moments of physical ecstasy. The first is when the soul of the dead yeshiva student enters the body of his beloved on her wedding day. The bride is consumed by him, her voice becomes his, her language becomes his and her body becomes his. But she struggles. She struggles against him as much as she wants him. He is fighting her and fucking her inside her own body.

This is taken even further when the rabbis attempt to cleave the soul of the dead man from the body of the living woman. A violent battle rages as the living and the dead continue to fight and fuck inside her. In our production, I had the dead student visibly present on stage, clinging to his beloved's body. The rabbis dowsed them with water, blew their ram's horns: Tekinh! Shvorim! Teruah! The two bodies, clothed in filthy underwear and drenched in cold water began the exorcism in a wheelbarrow full of dirty potatoes. Two screaming, deformed Siamese twins soon lay writhing and thrashing on the concrete floor. Two cockroaches scuttling and fucking among the wet potatoes.

One night was particularly cold. Freezing cold. The space was not heated. The audience were wrapped up in scarves, hats, gloves, coats and each other's horror. The two actors were virtually naked at the end of the exorcism. When they had been finally cleaved apart in a monstrous howl of separation, they made their way to a row of butcher's hooks, swinging behind them. On this winter's night, as they hung motionless and drenched on the hooks, steam rose from their wet, naked bodies. For a good three minutes, as another actor quietly recited the Kaddish prayer for the souls of the dead, this steam poured off the bodies of the two actors. A freak combination of room temperature and body temperature had produced one of the most beautiful things I have ever seen in the theatre. Slaughtered kosher meat steaming from glittering butcher's hooks.

> *The theatre, which is no thing, but*
> *makes use of everything—gestures,*
> *sound, words, screams, light, darkness—*
> *rediscovers itself at precisely the point*
> *where the mind requires a language*
> *to express its manifestations. To break*
> *through language in order to touch life is to*
> *create or re-create theatre.*
> Antonin Artaud

The theatre seems to me the perfect place for the ecstatic to manifest itself. Theatre is by its very nature an alchemical mix of manipulation, ritual and stimulation. Body, voice, light, sound. Who really knows what will be unleashed or unearthed when these forces combine. Or in what theatrical moments these forces will choose to emerge.

Many years after my *Dybbuk* production, I staged Ligeti's *Le Grande Macabre* in Berlin. The climax of the opera occurs when a gigantic meteor crashes into the earth. This has been foretold by a mad prophet, Nekrotzar. In Berlin, he sat on a white plastic toilet while a never-ending stream of brown excrement poured out of the toilet and over him. Ligeti's apocalyptically gorgeous music blasted out of the orchestra pit, as behind the toilet, half-dead hermaphroditic mermaids crawled across the stage, their glittering fins, sadly flicking in the air as they desperately searched for water, rest or salvation.

Many people in the audience found this scene offensive and tasteless. As if taste has anything to do with theatre. The baritone smeared himself with the excrement, ate it and sang. The more radiant the music became, the more he ate and smeared. I was, however, delighted that many people found this scene not tasteless, shocking or grotesque, but beautiful. As it was intended to be. Mountains of excrement, dying hermaphroditic mermaids and a baritone sitting on a toilet singing

Ligeti with shit all over his mouth may not be your average subscriber night at the opera, but something happened in the theatre at this moment. Something occurred. Something emerged.

It also emerged when Melita Jurisic killed her two children in my Vienna production of *Medea*. This act, by a woman driven to transgress one of life's most extreme taboos, must be a shocking moment. For the audience, that is. For Medea, it is something else. It should not be tender or contrite. It should not be mournful. It should not be full of self-pity. It should be a violent act of obscene power and terror. Something beyond the rational. Beyond self-control. Excessive. Violent. Ecstatic.

So when Melita Jurisic shoved her two small boys in a drawer, swung her axe and brought it down on the necks of her children, she unleashed a howl of pain, anger and exhilaration. It wasn't the axe, or the blood or the act of multiple decapitation. It was that howl, emerging from her cunt, through her body and out through her mouth. A visceral music born from somewhere else, emerging from her bloodstained, screaming mouth, travelling through the space where it entered our ears, sank into our bodies and transformed into something else. Something waiting to be born another time, something waiting to be touched by another sound, another imagination or another illumination.

IV

E cstasy in the theatre is best conveyed
through phantasmagoria. And the master of theatrical phantasmagoria is Wagner.
His theatre is a complex, shifting continent
where it really does become, for his characters and his audiences, very difficult to distinguish between what is real or imagined
and what is intended or hallucinated.

Der Fliegende Holländer is an opera in
which most of the characters spend at

least part of the drama asleep, daydreaming or hallucinating. In the very first minutes, Daland commands his men 'Lange war't ich wach: zu Ruhe den! Mir ist nicht bang!' (You've kept watch a long time: now get some rest! There's no more to fear!) and then goes below deck to sleep. The steersman can't even keep awake on his watch and soon falls asleep at the wheel, drowsily singing of his beloved. The Dutchman proclaims that he waits for the Day of Judgment when the dead will rise from their sleep. Senta daydreams at work and hallucinates at night. Erik dreams prophetic visions. No one in this opera seems to be wide awake, except perhaps the poor Dutchman, who seems to suffer from desperate and acute insomnia. Or is it just a case of extreme somnambulism? For the characters in *Der Fliegende Holländer* to achieve their state of ecstasy, they must first sleep. Then through their dreams they watch or witness. This witnessing takes the place of phantasmagoria, which then transforms itself into an ecstatic state.

The act of seeing is crucial in *Der Fliegende Holländer*. In my second attempt at the opera in Essen, we made the unrelenting voyeurism of the characters the key element in the production. When the curtain rose there was no water, no ship, no sailors. A 13-year-old girl in white underwear stood on a large rock in an otherwise empty white room. An enormous window behind her was closed off by a white curtain. When the curtain slowly opened, the audience saw through the large window an apartment building with more windows revealing many other rooms. In these rooms stood various groups of men, watching the girl through binoculars. It was unclear who was watching who. What act of voyeurism was taking place and, as often in Wagner's operas, whose dream is it, anyway? The Dutchman entered the empty white room through a hole in the wall, as if he were a burglar climbing into the young woman's space. Later, the young girl, Senta, was transformed into the older, singing version of herself, and was spun around the room like a whirling top during the spinning chorus.

At every opportunity, we sought to convey the disturbing impression of unseemly observation, of inappropriate perving. Daland showed the Dutchman polaroids of his daughter to persuade him to step ashore and take a wife. Senta even appeared in the opposite apartment building, watching herself in the empty white room. When the Dutchman finally appeared to her, the white curtains opened to reveal, not the building opposite, but a fertile, lush garden. Eden had appeared in her living room. Delirious with joy, she sings:

> Versank ich jetzt in wunderbares
>   Träumen?
> Was ich erblicke, ist's ein Wahn?
> ... Wei ich ihn oft gesehen, so steht er
>   hier.

(*Am I now deep in some wondrous
dream?
Is what I see a vision?
… He is here as I have often seen him.*)

Der Fliegende Holländer is a seasick phantasmagoria. Every bar is a further twisting of horror, frustration and rapture. When the action finally erupts in the wedding party and the appearance of the ghost ship chorus, the white room filled up with more than 150 identically dressed Sentas. Male, female, young, old. Doppelgänger after doppelgänger. The real Senta disappeared in a frenetic ocean of herself. At the climax of the scene, an old-man Senta gave birth to a skeleton of Senta, which the other Sentas proceeded to rape. The 150 Sentas ripped off their red dresses and hurled them onto the floor of the white room, like drops of splattered blood or fragments of ship's sails. It comes as no surprise when the first words uttered after this vision are:

Was muss ich sehen?
Ist's Taushung, Wahrheit? Ist es Tat?

(*Must I see this?*
Is this delusion or the truth?
Can it be?)

Senta, through ecstatic delirium, has willed the Dutchman into existence. Hitchcock's *Vertigo* meets Polanski's *Repulsion*. She is Jimmy Stewart, Kim

Novak and Catherine Deneuve all rolled into one.

So much of *Der Fliegende Holländer* is about reality set adrift in time and space. Time and space are the water. The characters search for shore, home, sanctuary, love and salvation in this Wagner ocean hallucination. There is no anchor. There is no shore. There is no home. At the end of our production, Senta slit the Dutchman's throat and sacrificed him on the rock in the middle of her room. At the end, she sat staring out into space with her slaughtered victim lying beside her. A look of elation and ecstasy glimmering from her eyes.

If *Der Fliegende Holländer* is about what the eye perceives, then *Lohengrin* is about how the ear transforms. *Lohengrin* is an opera about sound. No other stage work by Wagner contains so many references to hearing and calling. The entire dramatic crux of the opera hangs on the forbidden articulation of three questions. It opens with a herald calling on the citizens of Brabant to hear what King Heinrich has to say to them. The king then calls on Telramund to explain to him the malicious rumours he has heard from far away. Elsa is called for by name: 'Elsa, Ersheine heir zur Stell!' (Elsa, appear at this place!) All this calling, and we are only fifteen minutes into the opera.

The calling upon calling upon calling becomes clearer during Elsa's narration. Like Senta, she transcends relatively quickly into states of rapt enthralment. However, unlike Senta, Elsa hears things. In her first entrance, she is mute. The men question her. She remains silent, only nodding her answers. When she finally sings, as Wagner describes, 'Elsa's Mienen gehen von dem Ausdruck träumerischen Entrücktseins zu dem schwärmerischer Verklärunguber' (Elsa's expression goes from one of dreamlike detachment to one of frenzied transfiguration). In *Der Fliegende Holländer*, Senta sings about a man's portrait she stares at obsessively, day and night. Elsa's awakening occurs in an entirely different form. After the disappearance and presumed death of her brother Gottfried, she buries herself in lonely prayer. But something occurs as she pours out her grief.

Du drang aus meinem Stöhnen

ein Laut so klangevoll,

der zu gewalt'gem Tönen

weit in die Lüfte schwoll:

Ich hört ihn fernhin hallen,

bis kaum mein Ohr er traf;

mein Aug'ist zugefallen,

ich sank in süßen Schlaf.

(And from my groans

there issued a plaintive sound

that grew into a mighty roar

as it echoed through the skies:

I listened as it receded into the distance

until my ear could scarcely hear it;

my eyes closed

and I fell into a deep sleep.)

What an extraordinary process Elsa experiences. From the groans of her agony (expressed in the pious form of prayer) a sound is born. A tone. A plaintive tone. Melancholy. Her melancholy grows into a deafening echo and then retreats into a sound so soft it is almost imperceptible to the human ear. And then, and only then, does she fall into a sleep. Melancholy to echo to sleep. But unlike her colleagues in *Der Fliegende Holländer*, sleep offers Elsa no catalyst for her ecstasy. Sound is the trigger. We have already heard this process, but in reverse, in the orchestral prelude to the opera. The music begins with the strings, high and soft, almost imperceptible. Floating somewhere above something. In the first few pages of the score, the music descends, increasing in volume, and then dies out to nothing more than a vibrating echo. The prelude itself seems to be an echo of Elsa's trance. The figure of Lohengrin emerges from this echo. She sees only after she hears, a fact I pushed with tragic irony in my production of the opera at the Vienna Staatsoper. Elsa was blind in this production. Literal sight was an impossibility for her. She can see only in her imagination. Through an almost superhuman effort, she wills her beloved into life. Lohengrin is born from her groans. He is called by her echo. He is a sonic, Teutonic golem.

Before Lohengrin appears, the people of Brabant call out for him to make himself physically present. The herald calls.

The trumpets blare. The world waits with expectant anxiety. But he does not come. 'Ohn Antwort is der Ruf verhallt' (The call has died away unanswered) sing the men of Brabant. Elsa beseeches the king to call for her beloved once more: 'Wohl weilt er fern und hört' ihn nicht' (He is surely a long way off and could not hear). Once again the herald calls, once again the trumpets blare. Once again the world waits. And once again, he does not appear: 'In düstrem Schweigen richtet Gott' (In dismal silence God passes judgment). In a state of joyful, delirious transfiguration, Elsa calls on her beloved with a fanatical resolve in her own belief: 'La mich ihn sehn, wie ich ihn sah, wie ich ihn sah, sei er mir nah!' (Let me see him now as I saw

him then, as I saw him then, let him be
near me!) In Vienna, the chorus had to
physically restrain Elsa, so great and violent was her demand. Her messiah had
appeared to her once before in her dream.
He *must* answer her. He *must* appear now.
Sound *must* be metamorphosed into flesh.
In *Lohengrin*, this transformation appears
in gleaming silver armour, helmet, shield,
sword, golden horn, and is standing on
a boat pulled along the water by a white
swan. In my Vienna production there was
no shining armour, no boat and no swan.
The opera is not really about those things.
The chorus swirled around Elsa. Her
ecstasy became their ecstasy. They all saw
their own version of what she saw, like an
evangelical prayer meeting. At the climax

of their group ecstasy, they erupted all over the stage, furiously running and then leaving it empty, except for a man in a grey suit, sitting on a small wooden chair with his back to the audience. Lohengrin had appeared from her call, from her need for him to appear.

In the second act, the theme of hearing and calling is extended even further. Elsa tells the heavens that once they were filled with her sad laments, but now they will be filled only with the sounds of her happiness. When Ortrud calls her from the darkness, Elsa shudders: 'Wer ruft? Wie schauerlich und klagend ertönt mein Name durch die Nacht' (Who calls? How terrible and plaintive is the sound of my name as it rings out through the night). The calling of a name from the darkness by an unseen voice is an act that ricochets through almost every culture and mythology. It has a terrible power and for Elsa, it will lead to the disintegration of her vision. In Vienna, because Elsa was blind, Ortrud was able to deliberately confuse her by moving around and disorienting her sense of perception. Sound now becomes a weapon. Ortrud's voice, sliding through the darkness, is transformed into sonic poison.

In the third act love duet between Elsa and Lohengrin, they are only left alone when the sweet, sickly bridal song has faded into silence. Lohengrin even points out that now no eavesdropper will be able to hear their rapturous declarations of love. Strictly for their ears only. For Elsa, sound now is not enough. She wants to breathe in the delight that has been given to her. She wants to dissolve before his gaze, disappear into nothingness before his eyes. She wants to be like a stream of water winding around his feet or like a flower bowing towards him. Elsa, no longer content with her physical self, wants to undergo a series of transformations that will bring her closer and closer to her husband. She wants to become the phantasmagoria itself. Her love, 'unaussprechlich wonnevoll' (inexpressibly divine), cannot be named, just like Lohengrin. Later on, she even wishes to simply melt away in him.

He gently calls her name. Her request to hear his name carries with it a troubled erotic intensity:

Wie suß mein Name deinen Mund
   entgleitet!
Gönnst du des deinen holden Klang
   mir micht?
Nur, wenn zur Liebesstille wir geleitet,
Sollst du gestatten, daß mein Mund ihn
   spricht.
Einsam, wenn niemand wacht;
Nie sei der Welt er zu Gehör gebracht!

(*How sweet the sound of my name
   from your lips!
Will you not grant me the fair sound of
   yours?
Only when we lead to the stillness of
   love
Shall you allow my lips to pronounce it.
All alone when everyone is asleep;*

Never shall it be brought to the ears of the world.)

What an astonishing series of images Wagner presents here. Forbidden names, the silence of love, sound emerging from a lover's lips and the inability of the waking, real world to hear. Elsa, unable to control her quite reasonable curiosity, eventually asks the forbidden questions: Who are you? Where did you come from? What is your origin? And so she sets in motion the last section of the opera. By the end, Elsa's sounds have become a confused, horrible nightmare for her. More pompous fanfares, more bellowing male voices, more empty proclamations. Her hallucinations are cracking. Her dead brother returns (Or does he?), Lohengrin retreats (Or does he?) and the world she has created, given birth to from her first plaintive sound, echoes back to her, terrifying and relentless. In Vienna, Elsa was alone on stage at the end of the opera. She gripped herself like a tormented embryo, unable to return to the womb. Her hands pushed against her ears in a futile attempt to block out the noise. To block out the echo. To block out the sound.

> From the very first entry of the cellos I felt my heart contract . . . I was no longer of this world. At the very end I wandered aimlessly through the streets and when I got home I said nothing and asked to be alone. The song of ecstasy continued to vibrate within me the

whole night long, and when I woke up in the morning, I knew that the world was a changed place.

Bruno Walter's simple but beautiful recollection of his first experience with *Tristan and Isolde* captures perfectly what so many artists and audiences have felt since the opera's premiere in 1865. In this 'song of ecstasy', Wagner's obsessive fascination with sight, sound, touch, smell and taste achieves a stunning symbiosis. From the first to the last note, the opera is an almost continuous vibration, where what is the beginning and what is the end is no longer possible to define.

The action begins with Isolde coiled like a panther. She listens to a mocking, off-stage song and then bursts forth in a tirade of rage, anger and frustration that has no precedence or equal in any other Wagner opera. This is not the mono-hysteria of Senta or the trance hallucinations of Elsa. This is naked rage. Exposed muscle. The music tears through the text like a knife slashing meat. Isolde rails against her captors: she commands her hidden powers of sorcery to emerge from her breast; she demands that the winds stir up a tempest to sink her and everyone else on the ship in the deep ocean. In her fury she wants to wake the 'träumende Meer' (the dreaming sea) from its sleep and wreak vengeance on the world. For most of this act, Isolde swings wildly between rage, sarcasm and withering irony. She is the only female character in Wagner with a bone of irony in her body. It comes as a welcome relief.

In the preparation of the death potion and its subsequent last-minute substitution for the love potion, the ecstasy of taste first appears in the opera. What is intended as the bitter and resolute taste of death becomes the intoxicating and destabilising taste of love. Barely has Tristan gulped down his share when Isolde snatches the cup from him. Wagner's own stage directions provide a guide to one of the most breathtaking and ambiguous moments in the history of opera.

She drinks.
Then she throws the cup away.
Both, seized with awe, in the

greatest excitement, but motionless, gaze fixedly into each other's eyes, in which the expression of the defiance of death soon gives way to the glow of love.

Trembling seizes them, they clutch convulsively at their breasts and pass their hands over their foreheads. Then their eyes once again seek each other, drop in confusion, then fix themselves again on each other with increasing longing.

Well, you wouldn't want to drink and drive on that potion. Drinking induces motionlessness which then induces voyeurism which then induces physical seizures which then induces yearning. I have always found it fascinating that their gaze is so intense that they are unable to look into each other's eyes. What burning is at work here? What do they see in each other's eyes? Illumination? Reflection? Wagner takes his time with this moment. He slows everything. On one level, it comes as a release for the two protagonists, but on another level, it is merely an extension of the unfolding that has been at work since the very first bar of the opera. Isolde loses sense of where, who and what she is. She even questions if she is still living. And all the while, the music pulses, surges and erupts through their intoxication like wave after wave of sound crashing in on itself.

In the second act, all senses are at work. Isolde chastises her maid for hearing sounds in the darkness. Her maid tells her that she is deluded by her desire into hearing only what she wants to hear. Isolde is warned to be wary of King Mark's servant; he has eyes full of spite and stealth. When Tristan finally bursts into the scene, the two lovers embrace with an almost unbearable passionate intensity. Is it really you I feel? Is it really you I see? Is it you in my arms? Is it an illusion? The words tumble from their lips, the music rushing forth with such relentless intensity that the singers' voices are swept up in a tsunami of ecstatic questioning and groping. The night sinks down on them and they become bound together in one breath.

Bricht mein Blick sich
wonnerblindet,
erbleicht die Welt
mir ihrem Blenden.

Selbst dann
Bin ich die Welt:
Wonne-hehrstes Weben,
Liebe-heiligstes Leben,
Nie-wieder-Erwachens
Wahnlos
Hold bewusster Wunsch

(*My eyes grow dim,*
blinded with ecstasy,
The world and its vanities
fade away …

I myself am
the world:
supreme bliss of being,
life of holiest loving,
never more to awaken,
delusion free,
sweetly known desire.)

Ecstasy in *Tristan and Isolde* is an erotic weaving together of desire, transfiguration, obliteration, darkness and death. It is translucent night music. Although Wagner's textual metaphors are sometimes hard to stomach, the music is an entirely different matter. In this opera, the orchestra is not accompanying the ritual of ecstasy as in *Der Fliegende Holländer* or in *Lohengrin*. No, here it breathes through

the voices, it spins through them. This is
no landscape of music. This is a vortex of
notes. A black hole of sound. A collective
pulse. We are no longer of this world.

In the third act, delirium reigns. Ecstasy
has turned into a disease, a sickness, eating
away at Tristan's heart and soul. He dies in
Isolde's arms, dies in her gaze, dies in her
eyes. Her final declaration brings together
seeing, hearing, feeling, touching and tast-
ing in a rapturous outpouring of love. She
asks the other characters if they can see
Tristan's dead eyes opening; if they can
see his dead heart proudly swelling; if they
can see his mute lips, breathing. She alone
can hear the secret melody, so wonderful,
so tender, that pierces her body. This melody floats around her, it transforms into

wind, it transforms into sweet, heavenly perfume. She can smell the music. She wants to taste the music, to sip it, to drown in it, to die in its smell. Her eyes hear. Her ears smell. Her tongue hears and her soul touches.

In dem wogenden Schwall,
in dem tönenden Schall,
in des Welt-Atems
wehenden All—
ertrinken,
versinken—
unbewußt—
höchste Lust.

(*In the surging swell,*
in the ringing sound,

in the last wave
of the world's breath—
to drown,
to sink—
unconscious—
supreme bliss.)

In the end, this music can only be experienced. Interpretation fails. Words are useless. Recordings do it no justice. You have to see the melody emerge from deep within the singer's body. To hear the melody being born out of the singer's mouth. To touch the melody as it travels through space. To smell the melody as it floats around you. To taste the melody as it submerges into your own body. Echoing. Vibrating. Ecstatic.

Barrie Kosky was born in Melbourne and lives in Berlin.

Regarded as one of the most innovative and provocative directors of his generation, Barrie Kosky has created theatre and opera productions for many of the leading European and Australian theatre and opera houses.

He has directed productions for the Komische Oper and the Staatsoper Unter den Linden in Berlin, the Vienna Staatsoper, the Hannover Staatsoper, the Aalto Theater, Essen, the Berliner Ensemble and the Edinburgh International Festival.

From 2001–2005, he was the co-artistic director of the Schauspielhaus Vienna.

Barrie Kosky has created work for the Australian Opera, the Sydney Theatre Company, the Malthouse, the Melbourne International Festival and Elision.

In 1996, he was the artistic director of the Adelaide Festival, a festival widely regarded as one of the best cultural events ever staged in Australia.

Little Books on Big Themes

Blanche d'Alpuget ON LONGING
Germaine Greer ON RAGE
David Malouf ON EXPERIENCE

Forthcoming titles
Don Watson ON INDIGNATION
Malcolm Knox ON OBSESSION
Gay Bilson ON INDIGESTION
Anne Summers ON LUCK

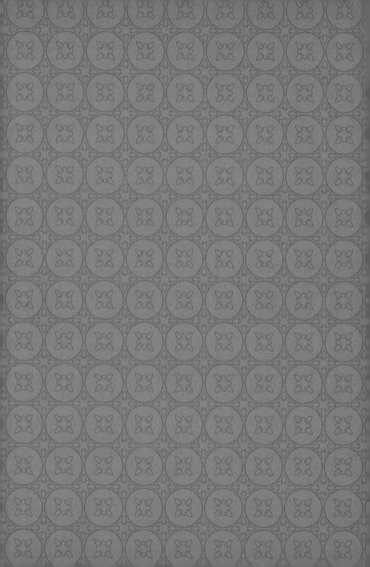